THROUGH WESLEY'S ENGLAND

T.E.Dowley, B.A., Ph.D.

Historical Consultant:

John A. Vickers, B.A., B.D., Ph.D.

Abingdon Press

Nashville

THROUGH WESLEY'S
ENGLAND

Copyright © 1988 by
Three's Company

ISBN 0-687-41899-2

Designed and created by
Three's Company
12 Flitcroft Street,
London WC2
Design: Peter Wyart
Typesetting by Goodwin
Press London
Worldwide co-edition
organized and produced by
Angus Hudson Ltd., London
Printed and bound by
Purnell Book Production
Limited, a member of
Maxwell Communication
Corporation

LIBRARY OF CONGRESS
Library of Congress
Cataloging-in-Publication
Data

Dowley, Tim.
    Through Wesley's
England/T.E. Dowley;
historical consultant,
    John A. Vickers.
        p.   cm.
    Includes index.
ISBN 0-687-41899-2 (pbk.)
    1. Wesley, John,
1703-1791—Homes and
haunts—England—Guide-
books. 2. Wesley, John,
1703-1791—Journeys—
England—Guide-books. 3.
England—Description and
travel—1971—Guide-books.
4. Methodist Church—
England. 5. Churches,
Anglican—England—Guide-
books. 6. Churches,
Methodist—England—Guide-
books. I Vickers, John A.
(John Ashley). II. Title BX
8495.W5D69 1988 287'.
092'4—dc19.
                        88-1906
                        CIP

Contents

80528

London

Bristol

Cornwall

The Midlands

Yorkshire

County Durham

John Wesley's Spiritual Journey   116

Introduction

John Wesley was the greatest traveller of his day within the British Isles. During his life he covered almost a quarter of a million miles, mostly on horseback, but in later life in a carriage. He continued travelling until his eighty-seventh year: 'I must be on horseback for life if I would be healthy.'

There are any number of manor houses, vicarages, farmhouses, inns and cottages where it is claimed that Wesley stayed. However, this little guidebook does not attempt to list the innumerable 'Wesley' trees, 'Wesley' chairs, 'Wesley' preaching places or bedrooms where Wesley slept a night. We have space here only to cover the major sites of importance to those who want to follow in the steps of the founder of Methodism.

We go first to Epworth, Wesley's birthplace; then to Oxford, his Alma Mater. We then look at the many places in London associated with John Wesley's life and ministry, before travelling west to Bristol, site of the first purpose-built Methodist preaching-house. Finally we visit places of interest to the Wesley pilgrim as far apart as Cornwall, Yorkshire and County Durham.

T.E.Dowley

John Wesley and his City Road Chapel, London.

John Wesley- founder of Methodism

John Wesley, the founder of Methodism, was the fifteenth child of Samuel and Susanna Wesley. His father was the High Church Rector of Epworth, then in Lincolnshire.

Saved from the burning rectory in 1709, John was sent to Charterhouse School in London, and then to Christ Church, Oxford, where he was later ordained and elected to a fellowship at Lincoln College.

The 'Holy Club'

After helping his father as curate in Epworth for a few years, he returned to Oxford, and joined his brother Charles and later the future preacher George Whitefield in a society which became nicknamed 'the Holy Club'. As well as prayer, meditation and Bible Study, this group also devoted itself to prison-visiting and other good works.

In 1635 the Wesley brothers were sent to North America by the Society for the Propagation of the Gospel. The mission was a personal and spiritual disaster.

> ❝I went to America to convert the Indians, but, oh, who shall convert me? ❞
> *John Wesley*

8

'Strangely warmed'

During the Atlantic voyage out, and when he returned to London in 1738, John Wesley was much impressed by the spirituality of German Moravian Christians. On 24 May 1738 his heart was 'strangely warmed' at an historic meeting in Aldersgate Street, London. He immediately went to tell his brother Charles: 'I believe!'

John Wesley was now set on his calling as an evangelist. He paid a short visit to the Moravian settlement at Herrnhut in Germany, then returned to England to commence his life's work of evangelizing the nation.

Field-preaching

In 1739 Wesley took a revolutionary step in his method of evangelism. At George Whitefield's prompting, John Wesley started to preach in the open-air - which remained the most effective means for the rest of his life. He preached in market-places, parks, commons, fields, and even pit-heads.

In this way he was able to reach the ordinary people, who otherwise might not have heard him 'offer Christ'.

Methodist societies

As believers increased in number, following his visits, Wesley began organizing them into 'societies', to prevent their falling away. These societies were grouped into 'circuits', which were in turn organized into 'districts'. The districts together formed the Methodist 'connexion'. Here were the roots of Methodism, although Wesley himself remained a loyal Anglican until the end of his life.

The effect of Wesley's preaching

“His countenance struck such an awful dread upon me before I heard him speak it made my heart beat like the pendulum of a clock, and when he did speak I thought his whole discourse was aimed at me. **”**
John Nelson

Travelling preacher

John Wesley spent his life riding the country on horseback, preaching the gospel. His main centres were London, Bristol and Newcastle-upon-Tyne, though he later extended his journeys into Scotland and Ireland too. He also sent preachers to North America, and in 1784 ordained Thomas Coke as superintendent of the work there.

John Wesley died in London in 1791 at the age of eighty-eight.

If a single soul falls into the abyss, whom I might have saved from the eternal flames, what excuse shall I make before God? That he did not belong to my parish? That is why I look upon all the world as my parish.
John Wesley

John Wesley

17 June 1703: Born at Epworth
9 February 1709: Rescued from fire at
Epworth Rectory
1714: Goes to Charterhouse School,
London
24 June 1720: Enters Christ Church,
Oxford
1725: Ordained Deacon
17 March 1726: Becomes Fellow
of Lincoln College, Oxford
1727: Holy Club first meets
1728: Ordained Priest
1735: Sails to Georgia
1738: Returns to England
24 May 1738: Evangelical conversion,
'heart strangely warmed'; Aldersgate
Street, London
2 April 1739: Commences open-air
preaching in Bristol
1739: Foundery opened in London
1742: Starts travels throughout England
25 June 1744: First Methodist Conference,
London
1751: Marries Mary Vazeille
1 November 1778: Opens City Road
Chapel, London
1 September 1784: Ordains two deacons
for North America
2 March 1791: Death in London

Charles Wesley (1707-88)

Charles Wesley was not simply a pale shadow of his older brother, John. It was Charles who started attending the 'Holy Club' at Oxford. He travelled to Georgia with John in 1735, and like his brother, experienced an evangelical conversion in 1738 which transformed his life: 'I now found myself at peace with God, and rejoiced in hope of loving Christ'.

Charles Wesley; detail from a portrait.

> **I now found myself at peace with God, and rejoiced in hope of loving Christ... I saw that by faith I stood; by the continual support of faith.**
> *Charles Wesley, Whit Sunday, 21 May 1738*

Evangelist

Charles was to become a great evangelist, field-preacher, Christian counsellor and pastor. For twenty years he travelled the length and breadth of the country preaching the gospel.

But he could not match the stamina of John Wesley, and settled down to live first in Bristol, later in London. He married Sarah Gwynne in 1749.

Even more than John, Charles Wesley was determined that the Methodist movement should not break away from the Church of England. He was a pillar of strength to his brother.

'Sweet singer' of Methodism

Above all, Charles Wesley is remembered as the 'poet of the Evangelical Revival'. A plaque outside his Bristol house proclaims that 'his hymns are the possession of the Christian Church'. They include such favourites as 'Love Divine, All Loves Excelling', 'Hark, the Herald Angels Sing', 'Christ the Lord is Risen Today', 'Jesu, Lover of My Soul' and 'O Thou Who Camest From Above'. It is reckoned that Charles Wesley wrote over 6,500 hymns in his lifetime; he dictated his last verses from his deathbed.

O For A Thousand Tongues To Sing

O for a thousand tongues to sing
    My dear Redeemer's praise,
The glories of my God and King,
    The triumphs of his grace!

Jesus! the name that charms our fears,
    That bids our sorrows cease;
'Tis music in the sinner's ears,
    'Tis life and health and peace.

He speaks; and, listening to his voice,
    New life the dead receive,
The mournful broken hearts rejoice,
    The humble poor believe.

Hear him, ye deaf; his praise, ye dumb,
    Your loosened tongues employ;
Ye blind, behold your Saviour come;
    And leap, ye lame, for joy!

My gracious Master and my God,
    Assist me to proclaim
And spread through all the earth abroad
    The honours of thy name.

Charles Wesley

Charles Wesley

18 December 1707: Born at Epworth
13 June 1726: Enters Christ Church, Oxford
1733: Introduces George Whitefield to the 'Holy Club'
September 1735: Ordained deacon and priest
1735: Sails to Georgia
December 1736: Returns to England
21 May 1738: Evangelical conversion, London
1748: Marries Sarah Gwynne
1771: Moves to London from Bristol
29 March 1788: Death

Wesley's England

- Edinburgh
- Newcastle-upon-Tyne
- Yarm
- Newbiggin
- Osmotherly
- Heptonstall
- **Epworth**
- Birmingham
- **Oxford**
- **Bristol**
- **London**
- Trewint
- Gwennap Pit

Epworth

John Wesley's birthplace

Although known throughout the world as Epworth, Lincolnshire, since 1975 Epworth has come within the new county of South Humberside. It is situated in the Isle of Axholme, an area west of the river Trent, once wooded and waterlogged, but drained by Dutch engineers in the seventeenth century.

Epworth is reached today along the A161 road from Gainsborough or Crowle.

John Wesley would still recognize Epworth's straggling High Street, the tree-lined path to Epworth parish church, and the Red Lion Inn.

An artist's impression of young John Wesley's rescue from the burning rectory at Epworth.

He visited Epworth every time he came to Lincolnshire, the last time only nine months before his death.

The Old Rectory, Epworth.

Epworth Rectory

The Old Rectory is reached from the centre of Epworth by walking past the Red Lion Inn and taking the winding road eastwards.

John Wesley was born in Epworth Rectory on 17 June 1703. The present rectory replaced his birthplace, a thatched building which was destroyed by fire in 1709. Young John was rescued from that blazing building by neighbours, 'a brand plucked out of the burning'.

Wesley describes the incident in his diary: 'I saw streaks of fire on the top of my room. I got up and ran to the door, but could get no further, all the floor beyond it being ablaze. I then climbed upon a desk which stood near to the window...'

John Wesley's father Samuel, rector of Epworth from 1695 until his death in 1735, rebuilt grandly; the new rectory, designed in Queen Anne style, cost him four hundred pounds and boasted fifty windows. This early eighteenth-century brick building has been restored to its original state by the World Methodist Council, who bought the house in 1954, with the generous financial help of Methodists throughout the world, particularly those from North America. The rectory was opened to the public as a Wesley museum in 1957.

Entrance hall

The interior has been carefully furnished as it might have appeared in Wesley's day.

In the entrance hall stands the original Wesley family sideboard, which has a history of its own. When Samuel Wesley died, the sideboard was sold to the landlord of Epworth's Red Lion Inn. It stood in the Red Lion for more than a century, before passing first to squire Adrian Peacock of Bottesford, and then to a Cheshire Methodist family. Finally it was bought back and restored to its original home in the Old Rectory.

Through double doors to the left of the entrance is the rectory parlour. Several windows in this room retain their original eighteenth-century glass.

To the right of the vestibule is the schoolroom where Mrs Wesley used to teach her young children for six hours a day, from nine o'clock till noon, and from two o'clock till five.

Kitchen
Passing through the schoolroom, we enter the kitchen, with its tiled floor, great open stepped chimney, and, hanging on the wall, the charred fragment of a wooden beam from the original rectory. The kitchen table is laid ready for a typical eighteenth-century meal.

Bedrooms
On the first floor of the rectory we find the bedrooms, including that of John's parents, where his mother, Susanna, retired each day to meditate and pray. At the end of the corridor is the little study where John Wesley's father, Samuel, prepared his sermons.

'Old Jeffrey's Chamber'
Narrow stairs lead to the attics, and to 'Old Jeffrey's Chamber', named after the family ghost. 'Old Jeffrey' made his presence known by strange rappings while the rector was at prayer, by the sound of breaking bottles and jingling coins, and sometimes by setting the handmill turning of its own accord. Even the family dog was affected by an invisible presence. Some people believe this was all the work of a poltergeist, perhaps set off by John's sister, Hetty, who was under considerable emotional stress.

St Andrew's Parish Church, Epworth

Opposite: St Andrew's Parish Church, Epworth. Samuel Wesley was rector here 1695-1735.

The parish church, where John's father Samuel Wesley served as rector for twenty-six years, was originally founded in the thirteenth century, and considerably damaged during the English Civil War. It can be reached from the Market Cross in the High Street via a stone-flagged avenue lined with lime trees.

The furniture

The church was renovated in 1868, when a new altar and pulpit were installed. However the sixteenth-century parish chest, two sixteenth-century chairs within the communion rail (one of these is said to have belonged to Susanna Wesley), and the eight-sided font where most of the Wesley children were baptized were all present in John Wesley's time.

The church also boasts a silver chalice, presented to Samuel Wesley by his patron, the Marquis of Normanby, in 1706, and from which young John received communion wine.

The parish register

Although the Epworth parish registers date back to 1538, when registration was first instituted in England, there is a gap between 1601-1710, so we have no entries for John and Charles Wesley's baptisms. There are, however, records of their sister Mary's marriage, and of their father Samuel's burial.

Still more interesting are the entries for 1727-29, since they are in John Wesley's own hand; he acted as curate to his father during this period.

Samuel Wesley's grave

Samuel Wesley's gravestone is found in the graveyard, and is reached along a pathway to the right of the south porch. Its original brickwork was replaced by stone in 1872, and two pieces of iron mark the place where John stood to preach in 1742, after being prevented from occupying his father's old pulpit by the officious curate in charge, the Revd John Romley.

The Revd Samuel Wesley's grave, Epworth churchyard.

Epworth Market Cross

A short distance along the High Street from the Wesley Memorial Chapel is the old market cross. A small plaque on the cross explains that John Wesley preached from here on a number of occasions.

The Red Lion Inn, Epworth

This public house, which overlooks the market square, was used by John Wesley several times when visiting Epworth, after his father's death. His first such visit was in 1742, when he preached to huge crowds from his father's tombstone for eight successive nights.

Foreground: Epworth Market Cross; background: The Red Lion Inn.

John Wesley preaches at Epworth

John Wesley preaches from his father's gravestone, Epworth; detail from a painting by George Washington Brownlow.

It being many years since I had been in Epworth before, I went to an inn, in the middle of the town, not knowing whether there were any left in it now who would not be ashamed of my acquaintance. But an old servant of my father's, with two or three poor women, presently found me out. I asked her, 'Do you know any in Epworth who are in earnest to be saved?' She answered, 'I am, by the grace of God; and I know I am saved through faith.' I asked, 'Have you then peace of God? Do you know that he has forgiven your sins?' She replied, 'I thank God, I know it well. And many here can say the same thing.'

Sunday 6th - A little before the service began, I went to Mr Romley, the curate, and offered to assist him either by preaching or reading prayers. But he did not care to accept of my assistance. The church was exceeding full in the afternoon, a rumour being spread that I was to preach. But the sermon on, 'Quench not the Spirit,' was not suitable to the expectation of the hearers. Mr Romley told them, one of the most dangerous ways of quenching the Spirit was by enthusiasm; and enlarged on the character of an enthusiast, in a very florid and oratorical manner. After sermon John Taylor stood in the churchyard, and gave notice, as the people were coming out, 'Mr Wesley, not being permitted to preach in the church, designs to preach here at six o'clock.'

Accordingly at six I came, and found such a congregation as I believe Epworth never saw before. I stood near the east end of the church, upon my father's tombstone, and cried, 'The kingdom of heaven is not meat and drink; but righteousness, and peace, and joy in the Holy Ghost.'

Wesley's Journal, 5/6 June 1742

27

Wesley Memorial Chapel, Epworth

This Methodist church was built in 1889, in neo-Gothic style and with a slim spire.

Its interior features simple pillars supporting an arched timber roof. Above the stained-glass window of the commissioning of the disciples is a fine replica of the Westminster Abbey medallion of John and Charles Wesley. Below this window is an oak screen and an old communion table, both from Epworth parish church. The Wesley family received the communion bread and wine from this table for many years. The oak font is a memorial to Susanna Wesley, while in the south transept there is a memorial tablet to John Wesley.

Wesley's advice to preachers

Endeavour to speak in public just as you do in common conversation...
To drawl is worse than to hurry.
The good and honourable actions of men should be described with a full and lofty accent; wicked and infamous actions, with a strong and earnest voice, and such a tone as expresses horror and desolation.
The mouth must never be turned awry; neither must you bite or lick your lips, or shrug your shoulders, or lean upon your elbow; all which give just offence to the spectators.
Never clap your hands, nor thump the pulpit.

OXFORD

In later years John Wesley declared: 'I love the very sight of Oxford.'

Christ Church

Like his brothers Samuel and Charles, John Wesley entered Oxford as an undergraduate at Christ Church, one of the grandest Oxford colleges. We do not now know which rooms he occupied in the college's huge quadrangle.

However, in the Great Hall, up the fine stone staircase with its fan-vaulted ceiling supported by a single pillar, there is a copy of Romney's famous portrait of John Wesley, believed to be by the artist himself.

Wesley's life at Oxford was full and varied. He met his friends at inns and coffee-houses, played billiards, backgammon, tennis and cards, went dancing, listened to music, took part in shooting and hunting, and even visited the theatre, horse races and the Bawtry Fair.

It was in the chapel of Christ Church, which is also a cathedral, that both John and Charles Wesley were later ordained priests in the Church of England by Bishop Potter.

Lincoln College

Following his ordination as deacon, John was appointed a Fellow of Lincoln College in 1726. This small college was founded in 1427, grew slowly, and in Wesley's day had a chapel and inner quadrangle.

Between 1727 and 1729 John returned to Epworth to assist his father as curate. Meanwhile his brother Charles, now up at Oxford himself, started to gather for prayer and Bible study with a little group of fellow students. When John returned to Oxford in 1729, he joined this group, nicknamed the 'Holy Club', and 'Methodists'. Other members of the group included George Whitefield, later to become a renowned preacher, and Benjamin Ingham.

Wesley's rooms
By tradition the rooms John Wesley occupied at Lincoln College are in the front quadrangle, where, in a blocked-up window, we can see a bronze bust copied from the one believed to be by Roubiliac, now in the National Portrait Gallery, London.

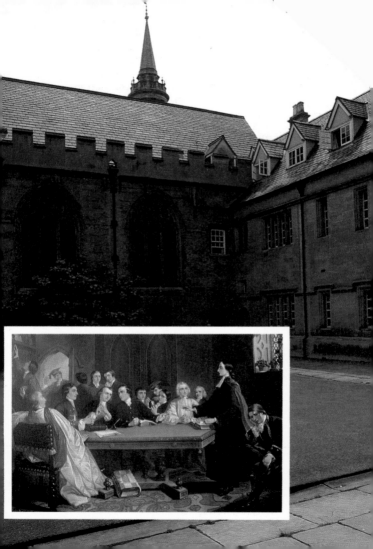

These rooms, which can be visited by arrangement with the college bursar, are on the first floor, up No. 2 staircase. They were restored in 1928 by the generosity of American Methodists. They feature antique linen-fold panelling, and old English furniture, including a mahogany writing-table, two Chippendale armchairs, a secretaire bookcase and a walnut bureau bookcase. None of this furniture is original to Wesley's time, but it lends a period atmosphere to the room.

A copy by W.D.Hamilton of Romney's portrait of John Wesley hangs on the wall. The original was finished when the sitter was eighty-five years old.

General Rules for Employing Time

1. Begin and end every day with God; and sleep not immoderately.
2. Be diligent in your calling.
3. Employ all spare hours in religion; as able.
4. All holy days.
5. Avoid drunkards and busy bodies.
6. Avoid curiosity, and all useless employments and knowledge.
7. Examine yourself every night.
8. Never on any account pass a day without setting aside at least an hour for devotion.
9. Avoid all manner of passion.

From John Wesley's diary, 1725.

Which rooms?

An Oxford historian, Dr V.H.H.Green, has questioned whether Wesley ever occupied these rooms: 'It seems impossible to say with absolute certainty who was living in them between 1729 and 1736, but it was certainly not John Wesley.' He claims that Wesley used, at different times, the two first-floor sets of rooms in the corner furthest from the chapel, on the Turl side of the Chapel quadrangle.

These rooms are less spacious and impressive than the restored rooms; but it was probably here that John Wesley first met with the Holy Club and began his daily discipline of prayer and Bible reading. However the existing 'Wesley Rooms' are a fitting memorial of John Wesley's connection with this college.

The Wesley Room, Lincoln College, Oxford, restored by the generosity of American Methodists.

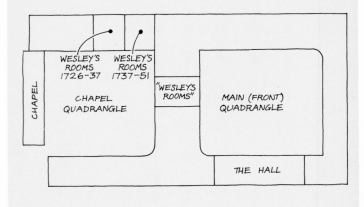

Plan to show where John Wesley lived in Lincoln College.

The chapel

The chapel of Lincoln College still houses the pulpit from which John Wesley preached during his years as Fellow of the college. It is a small building, with seven stained-glass windows, a black-and-white tiled floor and a shallow vaulted roof.

The college hall contains a portrait of Wesley, looking down from behind the high table. The college records include several references relating to Wesley, including the letter resigning his Fellowship, upon his marriage to Mary Vazeille in 1751 (a Fellow had to be unmarried).

The University Church of St Mary the Virgin

John Wesley preached the University Sermon at this church on seven occasions. It was in this historic church, too, that he won his first convert, Robin Griffiths, son of the vicar of Broadway, Gloucestershire. Here he also preached a sermon on Scriptural Christianity that so offended the authorities that he was never again invited to occupy this pulpit.

The University Church of St Mary the Virgin, Oxford.

St Michael's Church

This church was closely linked with Lincoln College. One of John Wesley's first duties as Fellow of Lincoln was to preach here, in 1726. A notice on the fifteenth-century pulpit commemorates that occasion.

Other Oxford churches

John Wesley preached in several other Oxford churches, including St Ebbe's, St Martin's, St Aldate's, St Thomas's and All Saints'.

The state of the nation

" Is there a nation under the sun, which is so deeply fallen from the very first principles of all religion? Where is the country in which is found so utter a disregard to even heathen morality, such a thorough contempt of justice and truth, and all that should be dear and honourable to rational creatures?... Such a complication of villainies of every kind, considered with all their aggravations, such a scorn of whatever bears the face of virtue, such injustice, fraud and falsehood; above all, such perjury, and such a method of law, we may defy the whole world to produce. **"**

John Wesley

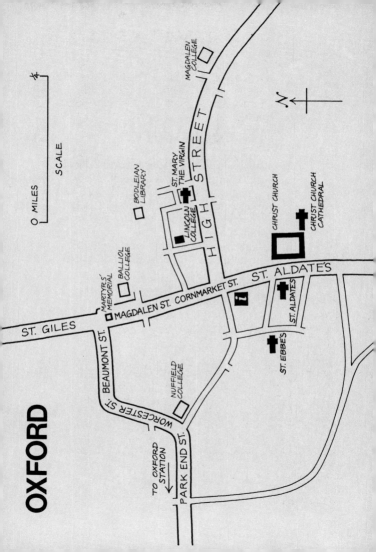

OXFORD

SCALE

0 MILES

N

MAGDALEN COLLEGE

HIGH STREET

ST. MARY THE VIRGIN

BODLEIAN LIBRARY

LINCOLN COLLEGE

CHRIST CHURCH

CHRIST CHURCH CATHEDRAL

BALLIOL COLLEGE

MARTYRS' MEMORIAL

ST. GILES

MAGDALEN ST.   CORNMARKET ST.   ST. ALDATE'S

i

ST. ALDATE'S

BEAUMONT ST.

NUFFIELD COLLEGE

ST. EBBES

WORCESTER ST.

TO OXFORD STATION

PARK END ST.

London

The Foundery

Wesley's first London headquarters
The Foundery stood off what is now Tabernacle
Street, near the City Road. It was within
shouting distance of Moorfields, where George
Whitefield and John Wesley practised field-
preaching.

Nothing remains of the original Foundery
building, which was a derelict arsenal when

True old Christianity

" I preached at Moorfields to about ten thousand, and at Kennington Common to, I believe,
near twenty thousand, on those words of the
calmer Jews to St Paul, 'We desire to hear of
thee what thou thinkest; for as concerning this
sect, we know that everywhere it is spoken
against.' At both places I described the real difference between what is generally called Christianity and the true old Christianity, which,
under the new name of Methodism, is now
also everywhere spoken against. **"**

Wesley's Journal, 16 September 1739

Wesley acquired it in 1739. Though the building was purchased for only £115, it cost a further £800 to repair it and to convert it into a suitable meeting-place for the Methodists.

Wesley fashioned from it a chapel holding 1,700 people, and a large room holding about 300, where sixty-six class meetings gathered each week. There was also a bookroom, a free school for sixty pupils, and a free dispensary. A preaching service was held in the Foundery at five o'clock every morning, and in 1744 the very first Methodist Conference was held there.

John Wesley lived in private rooms 'high up in the air' above the Foundery chapel. His mother, Susanna, spent her last years in these rooms, and died there.

The Foundery, Wesley's first London headquarters.

❝Lord, let me never live to be useless.❞
John Wesley

City Road Chapel

The lease on the Foundery ran out after forty years. By this time the Methodists were fighting a losing battle with the fabric of the old building, which leaked badly.

Wesley now acquired a one-acre site on the east side of the new City Road (then known as Royal Row), where he planned to build a new chapel. A condition in the lease required that the chapel be situated back from the road; this accounts for the spacious forecourt we see to-day.

City Road Chapel, London, opened in November 1778.

Stone-laying

On 21 April 1777, a stormy day, John Wesley laid the first stone of the new chapel, before a congregation of 2,000 from the Foundery

From John Wesley's letter of appeal to the
Methodist Societies, October 1776

"The Society at London have given
assistance to their brethren in various parts
of England. They have done this for upwards of thirty years; they have done it
cheerfully and liberally... They now stand in
need of assistance themselves. They are
under a necessity of building, as the
Foundery, with all the adjoining houses, is
shortly to be pulled down... I must
therefore beg the assistance of all our
brethren. Now help the parent Society,
which has helped others for so many years
so willingly and so largely. Now help me,
who account this as a kindness done to
myself; perhaps the last of this sort which I
shall ask of you. **"**

Chapel. He preached on the text: 'According to
this time it shall be said: What hath God
wrought' (Numbers 23:23).

Wesley set out to 'build an elegant chapel
such as even the Lord Mayor might attend',
and this made heavy demands on the finances
of the members. John and Charles Wesley
both toured the country in search of funds.

Opening
The chapel was built by Samuel Tooth, a local
preacher and class leader, and was finally
opened on 1 November 1778, although it was

not until 1779 that John Wesley took up occupation of the house built for him to the right of the chapel forecourt.

Wesley wrote in his journal of the new chapel: 'It is perfectly neat, but not fine; and contains far more people than the Foundery.' For the last twelve years of Wesley's life, this building was the spiritual centre of Methodism. It was in this chapel that the early Methodist Conferences took place, and the first Ecumenical Methodist Conference was held here in 1881. It remains a memorial to John Wesley, and as a place of worship sustains a living continuity with the founder of Methodism.

Saved from fire
City Road Chapel has three times been saved from destruction by fire. Only two years after its completion, John Wesley was woken at two o'clock in the morning by a blaze in a neighbouring timber-yard. He gave the alarm, and the chapel was saved.

A century later, in 1879, a policeman on night-duty noticed flames coming from the building. As a result of his prompt action, the chapel was largely saved, although the roof and fine ceiling were destroyed, and the sanctuary flooded. However, impressions were taken of what remained of the Adam-style ceiling, and a fine replica created to replace it.

During World War II, enemy bombs started fires all around, but the chapel itself was saved. On the night of the worst air-raids of the war, all the surrounding buildings were destroyed; Wesley's Chapel was saved by the heroism of firewatchers and firefighters, and because of a change in the wind-direction.

The Foundery Chapel

Wesley's Chapel itself remains substantially as it was in Wesley's day. The portico was added in 1815, and the Foundery Chapel (formerly called the Morning Chapel), to the right of the vestibule, was constructed in 1898, to provide a smaller place of prayer. It houses some of the old forms from the Foundery, the lectern from the Foundery bandroom, and Charles Wesley's own pipe-organ, similar to one made for the composer George Frideric Handel.

The Foundery Chapel, City Road Chapel. Charles Wesley's pipe-organ can be seen on the left.

> It pleased God to kindle a fire which I trust shall never be extinguished.
> *John Wesley, on The Awakening*

The Chapel

The main chapel originally had a double-decker pulpit some fifteen feet high. The precentor, who led the unaccompanied singing, sat at ground level; prayers were said from the first level; and the sermon was preached from the top. It is said that on one occasion Charles Wesley got so carried away with his preaching that he knocked the pulpit Bible down on the head of the unfortunate Dr Coke below! The pulpit was later reduced in height and the lower desk removed.

The gallery of the chapel was originally supported by pinewood from the masts of ships from the Deptford dockyards, given to Wesley by King George III. These pillars were covered with plaster and painted to give a marble effect. They were later replaced with French jasper columns given by Methodists from the

Charles
Wesley's pipe-
organ, in the
Foundery
Chapel.

The font at City Road Chapel originally belonged to John Fletcher's Church at Madeley.

United States, Canada, South Africa, Australia, the West Indies and Ireland. Some of the original old masts are still in use as pillars in the chapel vestibule.

In Wesley's time men and women sat separately, but this strict segregation ceased soon after he died.

The dove and serpent motif on the front of the gallery has been variously interpreted as a symbol of peace, of healing, of eternity, and of the Holy Spirit.

Furniture

The chapel's marble font came from John Fletcher's parish church at Madeley; the hollowed stone inside it from Nathaniel Gilbert's house in Antigua in the West Indies. The broken fetters carved into it remind us of the Methodists' fight against slavery. Gilbert preached to his own black slaves; from this stemmed the work of Methodist missions.

Renovations

In 1864 the lease expired, and the freehold was bought outright. In 1891, to mark the centenary of John Wesley's death, the building was renovated and the foundations reinforced. Meanwhile the once plain structure was gradually embellished with Victorian monuments and memorials. Stained-glass windows were donated by daughter Methodist churches, and a carved communion table covering by Methodists of the Isle of Man.

The back of Wesley's Chapel; the plateglass screen to the vestibule is clearly visible.

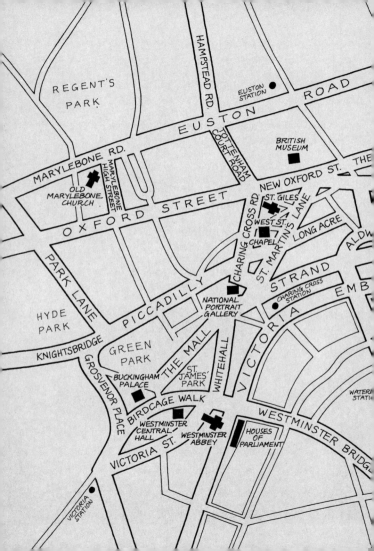

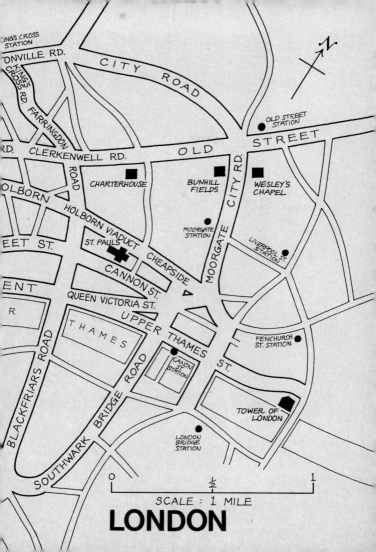

LONDON

Plaque to
Charles Wesley
in Wesley's City
Road Chapel.

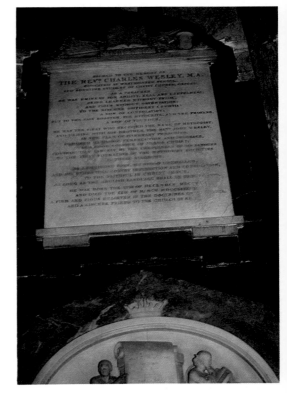

Restoration

Further major restoration was undertaken in the
1970s, by which time the chapel had become
so dilapidated that the local council had condemned it as unsafe for public use. The huge
amount of money needed to restore the chapel
was raised by Methodists from twenty-four
countries, but largely from Great Britain and

the United States. The chapel was re-opened by H.M. Queen Elizabeth II, on the bicentenary of the original opening, 1 November 1978, and in the presence of Methodists from all parts of the globe.

The sanctuary

As part of the restoration, a more spacious vestibule was created, with a plateglass screen affording a clear view of the chapel itself. A new sanctuary was created in front of the pulpit, while the old sanctuary, with its memorials of the Wesleys and other early Methodist leaders, including John Fletcher of Madeley, Joseph Benson, Dr Thomas Coke and Adam Clarke, remains in the apse behind the pulpit.

Wesley tablet

The marble tablet to John Wesley's memory has a globe at its centre to symbolize that the world was his parish. The inscription on it was composed by Dr John Whitehead, Wesley's personal physician, who practised nearby in Finsbury Square. It reads:

'A man in Learning and sincere Piety scarcely inferior to any. In Zeal, Ministerial Labours and extensive Usefulness Superior, perhaps, to all Since the days of St Paul. Regardless of Fatigue, personal Danger and Disgrace He went out into the highways and hedges Calling sinners to Repentance, and Publishing the Gospel of Peace.'

The Wesley statue

The statue of John Wesley in the forecourt of the chapel is a bronze by Adams-Acton. It was provided in 1891 by Methodists throughout the world, and shows him with one hand holding an open Bible, the other raised in blessing.

Wesley's burial

When John Wesley died, his body lay in state in the chapel, and was viewed by 10,000 people. His burial took place behind the chapel at five o'clock in the morning by lantern light, for fear of unmanageable crowds. Those who attended were given a biscuit embossed with his likeness.

The inscription on John Wesley's tomb, in the chapel graveyard.

The chapel graveyard

Behind the chapel is the well-maintained graveyard, where more than 5,000 bodies lie

To the Memory of
THE VENERABLE JOHN WESLEY, A.M.
Late Fellow of Lincoln College, OXFORD.

This GREAT LIGHT arose
(By the singular Providence of GOD)
To enlighten THESE NATIONS,
And to *revive, enforce,* and *defend,*
The Pure Apostolical DOCTRINES and PRACTICES of
THE PRIMITIVE CHURCH:
Which he continued to do, both by his WRITINGS and his LABOURS
For more than HALF A CENTURY:
And, to his inexpressible Joy,
Not only, beheld their INFLUENCE extending,
And their EFFICACY witness'd,
In the Hearts and Lives of MANY THOUSANDS,
As well in THE WESTERN WORLD as in THESE KINGDOMS:
But also far above all human Power of Expectation,
Liv'd to see PROVISION made by the singular Grace of GOD,
For their CONTINUANCE and ESTABLISHMENT,
TO THE JOY OF FUTURE GENERATIONS,

READER If thou art constrain'd to bless the INSTRUMENT,
GIVE GOD THE GLORY.

After having languished a few Days, He at length finished his COURSE and his LIFE together, Gloriously triumphing over DEATH March 2.
An. Dom. 1791. in the Eighty eighth Year of his Age.

THE WORLD IS MY PARISH.

buried. The ground is honeycombed with vaults and tombs containing lead coffins. Many of Wesleys preachers are buried near him; he declared: 'I should like to be buried here, and on the morning of the Resurrection rise with all my children round me.'

The original pulpit from the Foundery, now housed in the Museum of Methodism.

The Museum of Methodism

In the crypt beneath the chapel is the Museum of Methodism, opened in September 1984, which tells the story of the Wesleys and the worldwide movement they began. Outstanding exhibits include the original wooden pulpit from Wesley's Foundery Chapel, commemorative pottery, and a graphic display retelling the story of John and Charles Wesley. There is also a bookstall and souvenir shop.

Detail from a modern copy of a portrait of John Wesley.

Though I am always in haste, I am never in a hurry.
John Wesley

John Wesley's House

Opposite: John Wesley's house in City Road, next to Wesley's Chapel. The obelisk is a memorial to his mother, Susanna Wesley.

47 City Road, EC1

Wesley's tall, narrow house remains, although the manse, on the opposite side of the forecourt, is more recent. In Wesley's day there were stables and an old cottage to the left of the chapel. Dr Thomas Coke opened a bookroom in the cottage.

Wesley's last years

The death of John Wesley, by Marshall Claxton, R.A. See p.63 for a discussion of its authenticity.

In his last years, John Wesley spent the winter months at this London house, after it became ready for his occupation in October 1779. By this time he had given up horseback riding in favour of a simple horse-drawn carriage. Each spring his horses were brought from their winter quarters at Barnet, Hertfordshire, his

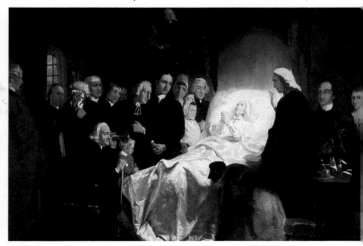

Wesley at eighty-five

This day I enter on my eighty-sixth year. I now find I grow old: 1. My sight is decayed; so that I cannot read a small print, unless in a strong light. 2. My strength is decayed; so that I walk much slower than I did some years since. 3. My memory of names, whether of persons or places, is decayed; till I stop a little to recollect them. What I should be afraid of, is, if I took thought for the morrow, that my body should weigh down my mind; and create either stubbornness, by the decrease of my understanding; or peevishness, by the increase of bodily infirmities: but thou shalt answer for me, O Lord my God.

Wesley's Journal, 28 June 1789

coach was repainted, and he set off once more on his travels.

Although in the winter of 1791 his health was weakening rapidly, John Wesley still made his usual preparations for the summer's travelling. He wrote in a faltering hand: 'I am half blind and half lame, but by the mercy of God, I creep on still.'

Ground floor

On the ground floor, to the right of the narrow hall, we find the parlour and a little dining room beyond.

The parlour is now the reception room of the museum, with a small bookstall. Among the interesting exhibits in this room is the preaching plan for January-April 1791; John Wesley's name appears for January and February, although he died in March of the same year.

The dining room, now called the Documents Room, displays further intriguing exhibits. American visitors will want to see the document dated 2 September 1784, appointing Thomas Coke as superintendent of the Methodist work in America. There is also an oil painting of Bishop Francis Asbury, the circuit rider ordained by Thomas Coke in Baltimore in 1784; and a letter to John Wesley from his mother, Susanna, addressed to 'Jacky'.

John Wesley's apartments

Wesley's personal apartments - a study, bedroom and tiny prayer room - are on the first floor of the house.

Wesley's letter commissioning Thomas Coke to superintend the Methodist work in North America, now on display in Wesley's House.

Wesley's study

The front room was his study. Here he wrote many of his numerous letters, transcribed his famous Journal, edited his books, and administered the growing Methodist movement.

We can see his walnut bureau, with its secret compartments, where he sat to work; his Chippendale bureau; and his bookcase, containing many of Wesley's personally annotated books. There is also the chair in which he sat for the historic first Methodist Conference at the Foundery.

Standing against the wall is John Wesley's long case clock, made in 1693 by Claudius du Chesne, and indicating the day of the month as well as the hour of the day. The unusual 'cockfighter's chair', or library straddle chair, with an adjustable back that can be used as a

John Wesley's 'cockfighter's chair'.

desk, and that provides pen and ink, was apparently given to Wesley by a converted bookmaker. Hanging on a stand is John Wesley's black brocade travelling-cloak, with his three-cornered hat, preaching tabs, and his silver-buckled shoes.

The modern portrait of John Wesley over the fireplace is by Frank O.Salisbury, and was based on a contemporary bust by Enoch Wood.

John Wesley's study and his Chippendale bureau.

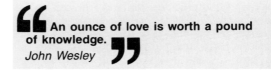

"An ounce of love is worth a pound of knowledge.

John Wesley

John Wesley's bedroom; it is possible that he died in this room in 1791.

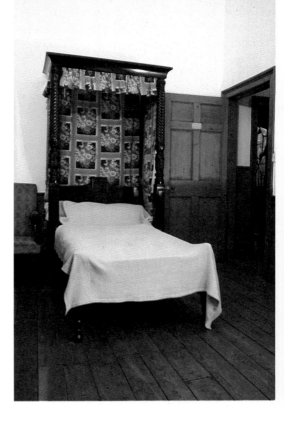

Wesley's bedroom

Behind the study is Wesley's little bedroom, measuring only fourteen feet by eleven. The bed, although of the period, is not Wesley's original. There are also two glass-fronted wall cupboards, a chest-of-drawers, an armchair and Wesley's bedside table.

John Wesley possibly died in this room, aged eighty-eight, on 2 March 1791. In the room is a print of Marshall Claxton's romanticized painting 'The Death Bed of Wesley', with a key identifying the crowd of visitors surrounding the dying preacher. Clearly all these people could not have been present together in such a small room!

Wesley's prayer room

From the little bedroom we enter the yet smaller prayer room, only seven feet by eight, but sometimes called the 'powerhouse of Methodism'. Here John Wesley said his morning prayers, rising at four o'clock almost until his death: 'Here then I am far from the busy ways of man. I sit down alone; only God is here. In his presence I open, I read his Book.'

The only furniture in here is a chair, a prayer stool, a Queen Anne table on cabriole legs and a metal candle-holder. The fireplace dates from Wesley's time.

The second floor

In Wesley's time, the second floor of the building housed Wesley's fellow preachers.

The museum room

Today the front room on the second floor houses further Wesley mementoes, and is known as the Museum Room. Here we find John Wesley's reading glasses, a candle lantern from his coach, his last quill pen, his spurs, and his cup and saucer. Other fascinating objects are found in the glass-fronted cupboards, including plaques, cups, and commemorative Staffordshireware, much of it decorated with portraits of Wesley.

The huge Wedgwood gallon teapot was made specially for John Wesley as a gift from Josiah Wedgwood, and was used daily by Wesley and his preachers.

Another curiosity is the electrical machine, which Wesley used in his dispensary for the treatment of nervous illnesses. A current of electricity is produced by turning the machine's handle.

Wesley electrifies a patient

❝ I advised one who had been troubled many years with a stubborn paralytic disorder, to try a new remedy. Accordingly, she was electrified, and found immediate help. By the same means I have known two persons cured of an inveterate pain in the stomach; and another of a pain in his side, which he had had ever since he was a child. Nevertheless, who can wonder that many gentlemen of the faculty, as well as their good friends, the apothecaries, decry a medicine so shockingly cheap and easy, as much as they do quicksilver and tar-water? ❞

Wesley's Journal, 20 January 1753

John Wesley's advice to his preachers
Labour to avoid the odious custom of coughing and spitting while you are speaking. And if at some times you cannot wholly avoid it, yet take care you do not stop in the middle of a sentence, but only at such times as will least interrupt the sense of what you are delivering.

Wesley's cure for baldness
Rub your scalp with honey and onions, and electrify daily.

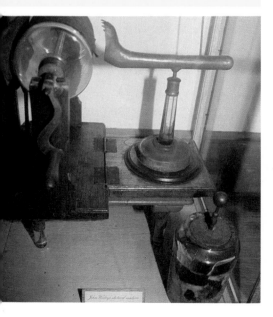

Wesley's electrical machine, for treating nervous illnesses.

Charles Wesley's room

In the back room on the second floor, Charles Wesley's room, we find mementoes of John's brother, Charles. The contents include his bureau, his study chair and his hymn book together with manuscripts of hymns in his own handwriting.

Bunhill Fields

In this famous Nonconformist burial ground, opposite Wesley's Chapel, we find the tomb of Susanna Wesley, John's and Charles' mother. The tomb is beside the left-hand path. The present gravestone was erected in 1828, and restored in 1978, with support from the Susanna Wesley Sunday School Class, Frederick, Maryland, USA.

The burial ground also contains the graves of Daniel Defoe, author of 'Robinson Crusoe', Isaac Watts, the hymnwriter, William Blake, writer of 'Jerusalem', and John Bunyan, author of 'Pilgrim's Progress'.

Susanna Wesley's tombstone, Bunhill Fields, London.

Love Divine, All Loves Excelling

Love divine, all loves excelling,
    Joy of heaven, to earth come down,
Fix in us thy humble dwelling,
    All thy faithful mercies crown.
Jesus, thou art all compassion,
    Pure, unbounded love thou art;
Visit us with thy salvation,
    Enter every longing heart.

Come, almighty to deliver,
    Let us all thy life receive;
Suddenly return, and never,
    Never more thy temples leave.
Thee we would be always blessing,
    Serve thee as thy hosts above,
Pray, and praise thee, without ceasing,
    Glory in thy perfect love.

Finish then thy new creation:
    Pure and spotless may we be;
Let us see thy great salvation,
    Perfectly restored in thee.
Changed from glory into glory,
    Till in heaven we take our place,
Till we cast our crowns before thee,
    Lost in wonder, love, and praise.

Charles Wesley

Other London Sites

Aldersgate Street, EC1

It was in a room in Aldersgate Street that John Wesley felt his heart 'strangely warmed' on 24 May 1738. Careful research has shown that Nettleton Court, where Wesley sat listening to a reading of Luther's preface to the Letter to the Romans on that memorable evening, was close to the present entrance to the Museum of London.

Memorial

An impressive new memorial, dedicated on 24 May 1981, now stands on the nearby raised walkway. It is said to represent 'the wind and fire of the Spirit', and features a copy of Wesley's account of his conversion experience taken from his Journal. It was just below this spot that Wesley experienced this, some two hundred and fifty years ago.

Plaque

A plaque, originally on the wall of Barclay's Bank, is now set into a low wall at the junction of Aldersgate Street and London Wall. It was provided by Drew Theological Seminary, now Drew University, New Jersey, USA.

Across the road, close to the site of Aldersgate, is another plaque, fastened to the railing of St Botolph's churchyard. Inside St Botolph's Church there is a stained-glass window depicting John Wesley preaching in nearby Moorfields.

Wesley's conversion

> 6 6 I went very unwillingly to a society in Aldersgate Street, where one was reading Luther's preface to the Epistle to the Romans. About a quarter before nine, while he was describing the change which God works in the heart through faith in Christ, I felt my heart strangely warmed. I felt I did trust Christ, Christ alone, for salvation; and an assurance was given me that he had taken away my sins, even mine, and saved me from the law of sin and death. 9 9

John Wesley, May 24 1738

The impressive memorial to Wesley's Aldersgate Street conversion experience.

Charterhouse, EC1

John Wesley entered Charterhouse School at the tender age of ten. He complained that he 'had but little bread to eat, and not great plenty of that'. However he later claimed that this 'laid the foundation of lasting health'. Each morning he ran three times round the school green for exercise, as his father had instructed him.

It was while at Charterhouse School that John Wesley gained his knowledge of Latin and Greek, as well as his lifelong interest in mathematics and natural science.

The school moved to Godalming in Surrey in 1872, and the school buildings disappeared. Parts of Charterhouse, originally a Carthusian monastery, survive, including the Great Hall, the fifteenth-century gateway and part of the

Charterhouse, London EC1.

Wesley preaches to the condemned

" I preached the condemned criminals' sermon in Newgate. Forty-seven were under sentence of death. While they were coming in, there was something very awful in the clink of their chains. But no sound was heard, either from them or the crowded audience, after the text was named, 'There is joy in heaven over one sinner that repenteth, more than over ninety and nine just persons, that need not repentance.' The power of the Lord was eminently present, and most of the prisoners were in tears. A few days after, twenty of them died at once, five of whom died in peace. **"**

Wesley's Journal, 26 December 1785

old priory, as well as the old chapel where Wesley worshipped as a schoolboy.

The buildings are normally open to the public only on Wednesday afternoons from April to July. A plaque commemorating Wesley is found in the cloisters.

Site of All Hallows Church, EC3

It was in this city church, near the junction of Gracechurch Street and Lombard Street, that John Wesley first preached extempore in 1735.

A woman apparently noticed his agitation as he turned back from the pulpit, realizing that he had left his sermon notes behind. She asked him: 'Cannot you trust God for a sermon?' Wesley reminisced: 'The question had such an effect upon me that I ascended the pulpit, preached extempore, with great freedom to myself and·acceptance to the people; and have never since taken a written sermon into the pulpit.'

All Hallows was demolished earlier in the twentieth century; the site is now occupied by the headquarters of Barclays Bank. A glass screen inside the bank commemorates this incident, as well as other local historic events.

Westminster School, SW1

While John was at Charterhouse, his brother Charles became a pupil at Westminster School. This historic school is situated under the shadow of Westminster Abbey, off Dean's Yard. Samuel Wesley, their older brother, was an usher at the school, and kept an eye on both boys. In 1725 Charles became school captain.

> **❝ I have only one point of view - to promote, so far as I am able, vital, practical religion; and by the grace of God, beget, preserve and increase the life of God in the soul of men. ❞**
> *John Wesley*

Indecency at St Paul's

St Paul's Cathedral; Wesley, an ordained Anglican, often worshipped here.

❝I wonder at those who talk so loud of the indecency of field-preaching. The highest indecency is in St Paul's Cathedral, when a considerable part of the congregation are asleep, or talking, or looking about, not minding a word the preacher says. On the other hand, there is the highest decency in a churchyard or field, when the whole congregation behave and look as if they saw the Judge of all, and heard him speaking from heaven.❞

Wesley's Journal, 28 August 1748

Opposite: The
memorial
medallion to
John and
Charles Wesley,
Westminster
Abbey.

Westminster Abbey

There is a memorial medallion to John and
Charles Wesley on the south side of the south
aisle of Westminster Abbey, designed by
Adams-Acton.

A statue of John Wesley by Samuel Manning
intended for the abbey was turned away by the
authorities, and now stands at the top of the
grand staircase of Westminster Central Hall,
across the road from the abbey.

Westminster Central Hall

Designed by the architect A.B.Rickards,
Westminster Central Hall was built early in the
twentieth century as a major Methodist church
for the capital. It is an impressive neo-baroque
building, with an internal grand staircase, and
an imposing dome that has become a familiar
feature of London's skyline. Its most famous
minister was W.E.Sangster (1939-1955), whose
wartime ministry was particularly valued.

The National Portrait Gallery, Trafalgar Square

The portrait gallery has on display the well-
known portrait of John Wesley by Nathaniel
Hone, painted about 1742. The gallery
possesses other Wesley portraits, and paintings
of his contemporaries, as well as a life-size
marble bust, possibly by Roubiliac.

JOHN WESLEY, M.A.
BORN JUNE 17, 1703; DIED MARCH 2, 1791.

CHARLES WESLEY, M.A.
BORN DECEMBER 18, 1708; DIED MARCH 29, 1788.

"THE BEST OF ALL IS, GOD IS WITH US."

"I LOOK UPON ALL THE WORLD AS MY PARISH."

"GOD BURIES HIS WORKMEN, BUT CARRIES ON HIS WORK."

West Street Chapel, WC2

This building, now 26 West Street, and not used as a church since it was bombed during World War 2, was Wesley's first Methodist church in the West End of London. Its origins as a chapel are clear from its arched windows and plain front.

John Wesley leased this chapel from the church of St Clement Danes for thirty pounds a year from 1743. It was renovated in 1759, and the lease renewed several times.

During the second half of the eighteenth century, the chapel was frequently crowded with Methodist worshippers. So many wanted to attend Wesley's opening service here that he continued preaching from ten o'clock in the morning until three in the afternoon, admitting the congregation in relays.

West Street Chapel, Wesley's first Methodist church in London's West End.

Since the chapel was a consecrated building, here, for the first time, Methodists could receive communion in their own place of worship. Not only John Wesley, but also Charles Wesley, George Whitefield and the saintly John Fletcher of Madeley preached from the pulpit of this chapel.

The Methodists gave up the chapel in 1798, when its activities were transferred first to Great Queen Street, Covent Garden, and later to Hinde Street Chapel and to Kingsway Hall. A blue plaque recording its early Methodist associations is now fixed outside the building, which has recently been adapted for use as a ballet school by the London City Ballet.

Wesley on riches

“ I fear, wherever riches have increased, the essence of religion has decreased in the same proportion. Therefore I do not see how it is possible, in the nature of things, for any renewal of true religion to continue long. For religion must necessarily produce both industry and frugality, and these cannot but produce riches. But as riches increase, so will pride, anger and the love of the world... **”**

“ Be never unemployed; be never triflingly employed. **”**

John Wesley

The West Street Chapel pulpit, now in the church of St Giles-in-the-Fields.

St Giles-in-the-Fields, WC2

Preserved in the north aisle of this splendidly-restored early eighteenth-century church is a green-and-white painted deal pulpit, which is the top section of Wesley's three-decker pulpit from West Street Chapel.

Old Marylebone Churchyard, NW1

Charles Wesley is buried in the graveyard of Old Marylebone Church, where his parents Samuel and Susanna had been married in 1688. In the graveyard stands an obelisk in memory of Charles, Sarah and their two sons, erected by the Methodist Conference in 1858.

Charles lived and died in nearby Great Chesterfield Street, now Wheatley Street, where the site is marked by a plaque on the King's Head public house. His widow long outlived him, and died in 1822 at the age of ninety-six.

Mission House, 25 Marylebone Road, NW1

This building has housed the headquarters of the Methodist Missionary Society since 1946.

Many historic portraits may be found in the building, especially on the first two stairways and landings, and in committee room A, on the first floor. These include two paintings of John Wesley, and others of Charles Wesley, Thomas Coke, Francis Asbury and Jabez Bunting, the nineteenth-century Methodist administrator

Westminster Central Hall, London.

The New Room,
Bristol, the
oldest
Methodist
preaching-
house in the
world.

Bristol

After London, Bristol was John Wesley's main centre. For the first thirty years of the Evangelical Revival he spent more time here than anywhere else.

John Wesley made his headquarters in the Horsefair, in the old part of the city. This was severely bombed during World War 2, and has since been rebuilt as a modern shopping-centre.

The New Room

The New Room, the oldest Methodist preaching-house in the world, survived the bombing, and still stands tucked in among the modern shops of Bristol. In Wesley's day it served as an active community centre - a bookshop, hostel, school, and dispensary, as well as a place of worship. Today it welcomes visitors from across the world, and acts as a reminder of the beginnings of Methodism.

The most unspoiled of Methodist shrines, the New Room preserves both its original form and its original atmosphere. It was built in 1739, reconstructed in 1748, and became the first Methodist building to be licensed officially for public worship.

❝God buries his workmen, but carries on his work.❞
Charles Wesley

The interior of the New Room retains its original form and atmosphere.

The chapel
Although the building remains largely as it appeared in the eighteenth century, the original backless forms were replaced early in the nineteenth century with the present pews, and the upper part of the pulpit was rebuilt.

The chapel, with its double-decker pulpit and gallery resting on sturdy columns, is attractive in its simplicity. John and Charles Wesley, John Fletcher, Dr Coke and every other early leader of the Revival preached from this pulpit.

First class-meeting
It was in the New Room that the Methodist class-meeting originated. It was suggested that each member be asked to give one penny towards paying off the society's debts. Because some members were too poor to afford this, a Captain Foy suggested that eleven members join a group with him, promising that he would make up any shortfall in their contributions. John Wesley quickly saw the value of such a system, and the class meeting soon became a central feature of Methodist spirituality and discipline.

John Wesley preaches in a dwelling-house, from an original painting at City Road.

Historic events

The second Methodist Conference also met at the New Room, and consisted of eleven leaders of the young movement. It was at a later Conference, in 1771, that a young preacher from the Black Country, Francis Asbury, volunteered to take the message of the Revival to North America.

Horseback statue

In the forecourt to the chapel stands a fine horseback statue of John Wesley, by Gordon A.Walker, R.A. The loose rein of the horse and the open book in the preacher's hand both symbolize aspects of Wesley's character. Behind the equestrian statue is the little whitewashed stable where Wesley would have kept his horse.

A statuette of one of Wesley's North American circuit-riders.

Living quarters

Above the chapel are the living quarters used by John Wesley and his household. They are reached via the gallery of the chapel. There is a central common room with a lantern window through which the chapel can be viewed.

Riot at Bristol

“ While I was expounding the former part of the twenty-third chapter of the Acts (how wonderfully suited to the occasion! though not by my choice), the floods began to lift up their voice. Some or other of the children of Belial had laboured to disturb us several nights before: but now it seemed as if all the host of the aliens were come together with one consent. Not only the court and the alleys, but all the street, upwards and downwards, was filled with people, shouting, cursing and swearing, and ready to swallow the ground with fierceness and rage. The mayor sent order that they should disperse. But they set him at nought. The chief constable came next in person, who was, till then, sufficiently prejudiced against us. But they insulted him also in so gross a manner, as I believe fully opened his eyes. At length the mayor sent several of his officers, who took the ringleaders into custody, and did not go till all the rest were dispersed. Surely he hath been to us 'the minister of God for good'. **”**

Wesley's Journal, 1 April 1740

Bedrooms

Opening from this room are the bedrooms, with John Wesley's in the far corner. His room has a desk fitted to the window sill. Portraits of John Wesley, Mrs Charles Wesley, John Fletcher and other early Methodist leaders are all on display, as well as John Wesley's bed, brought here from Kingswood School.

Wesley's household in Bristol included a housekeeper, maids, and often a schoolmaster and orphan children, in addition to Wesley's fellow preachers, who came and went constantly.

The large window-sill which Wesley used as a desk in his bedroom at the New Room.

❝ The best of all is, God is with us! ❞
John Wesley

Opposite: The imposing statue of Charles Wesley, in the courtyard to the New Room, Bristol.

Wesley's advice

Do all the good you can,
By all the means you can,
In all the ways you can,
In all the places you can,
At all the times you can,
To all the people you can,
As long as ever you can.

John Wesley

Charles Wesley statue

In the courtyard below stands a life-size bronze statue of Charles Wesley, his right hand characteristically outstretched, commending his Saviour.

Charles Wesley's House

For twenty-two years Charles Wesley lived at 4, Charles Street, not far from the Horsefair. It is one of two tall brick houses.

The front rooms retain their original Adam grates, and the house is furnished in period style. Original panelling remains in the hall and adjoining rooms. It is said that Charles Wesley composed many of his 6,000 hymns in the front attic of this house.

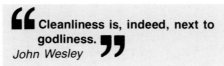

Cleanliness is, indeed, next to godliness.
John Wesley

Wesley meets a singer in Bristol

“ I light upon a poor, pretty, fluttering thing, lately come from Ireland, and going to be a singer at the play-house. She went in the evening to the chapel, and thence to the watch-night, and was almost persuaded to be a Christian. Her convictions continued strong for a few days; but then her old acquaintance found her, and we saw her no more. **”**

Wesley's Journal, 30 May 1746

Kingswood

Wesley's first approach to Bristol was through Kingswood, four miles east of the city. In his day it had a rough population of miners. No field of evangelism was less promising or offered stronger contrast with Wesley's own background. Yet it was here that his greatest work was done; the impact of his preaching was astonishing.

“ I could scarce reconcile myself at first to this strange way of preaching in the fields... having been all my life (till very lately) so tenacious of every point relating to decency and order, that I should have thought the saving of souls almost a sin if it had not been done in a church. **”**

Opposite:
Charles
Wesley's House;
4, Charles
Street, Bristol.

Hanham Mount

Hanham Mount, approached from Mount Hill Road, features a flagged cross marking the spot where the field-preachers once stood. The mount is topped by a beacon sixty-five feet high, which sends out a green light over the surrounding countryside.

At the base of the beacon is the inscription: 'Out of the Wood came Light'. One of the two bronze plaques on the beacon reads: 'On the Mount at the end of this path George Whitefield and John Wesley preached their earliest open-air sermons in A.D. 1739.' There follow two quotations from Wesley's Journal, and then the words: 'Church or no Church, we must attend to the saving of souls.'

Eastwards from the beacon is a flagged path along the mount, leading to a replica of Wesley's school pulpit, dedicated in 1983. In the paved area below stands a stone font brought here from Wesley's demolished school chapel, and bearing the words 'All the World is my Parish.'

Dr Johnson on Wesley's company

❝ John Wesley's conversation is good, but he is never at leisure. He is always obliged to go at a certain hour. This is very disagreeable to a man who loves to fold his legs and have out his talk, as I do. ❞

" There was great expectation at Bath of what a noted man was to do to me there; and I was much entreated not to preach, because no one knew what might happen. By this report I also gained a much larger audience, among whom were many of the rich and great. I told them plainly, the Scripture had concluded them all under sin - high and low, rich and poor, one with another. Many of them seemed to be a little surprised, and were sinking apace into seriousness, when their champion appeared, and coming close to me, asked by what authority I did these things.

I replied, 'By the authority of Jesus Christ, conveyed to me by the Archbishop of Canterbury...' He said, 'This is contrary to Act of Parliament... and beside, your preaching frightens people out of their wits.'

'Sir, did you ever hear me preach?' 'No.' 'How, then, can you judge of what you never heard?' 'Sir, by common report.' 'Common report is not enough. Give me leave, Sir, to ask, Is not your name Nash?' 'My name is Nash.' 'Sir, I dare not judge of you by common report: I think it is not enough to judge by.' Here he paused awhile, and, having recovered himself, said, 'I desire to know what this people comes here for'; on which one replied, 'Sir, leave him to me: let an old woman answer him. You, Mr Nash, take care of your body; we take care of our souls; and for the food of our souls we come here.' He replied not a word, but walked away. **"**

Wesley's Journal, 5 June 1739

Opposite:
Coverack
Wesleyan
Chapel,
Cornwall; a
typical English
rural Methodist
chapel.

Cornwall

Cornwall abounds in Methodist associations; there is hardly a market-place in the county where Wesley did not stand and preach. John Wesley paid a total of thirty-two visits to this county during his ministry.

Digory Isbell's Cottage,

Trewint, Bodmin Moor

Digory Isbell's
Cottage,
Trewint,
Cornwall.

This cottage was rescued from demolition in 1947, and subsequently restored to its original appearance. With its period furniture, it now looks much as it did when John Wesley knew it.

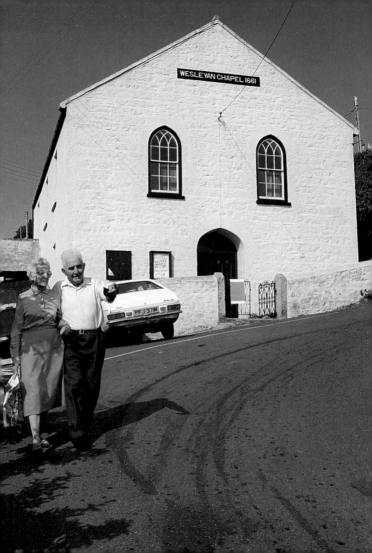

Opposite: John
Wesley at the
age of eighty-
six.

Wesley first came across the cottage when
travelling with two fellow preachers, with only
one horse between them. They took turns
riding, slept on hard boards, and lived off
blackberries. Wesley's travelling companions
knocked at the door of this cottage, and were
given bread, butter, and milk for themselves
and hay for their horse.

When Wesley himself visited the cottage, the
owner, Digory Isbell, doubted he was real:
'They do say in thaise parts yu baint John
Wesley at all - they reckon he died years
agone - but I dunnaw.' Nevertheless Digory invited his neighbours to come to hear Wesley
preach.

Wesley's rooms

One day, as Digory was reading his Bible, he
came to the story of the Shunammite woman
who built a room for the use of the prophet
Elisha. Digory decided to do the same for John
Wesley. He added two small rooms to his cottage, for the use of the itinerant preacher. Today a custodian lives in Digory's house, and
Wesley's rooms are open to visitors.

The smaller of the two rooms, which is
floored with Cornish slate, is still used for services. Above this room, and reached by an oak
staircase, is Wesley's bedroom. The preachers'
stable is now used as a bathroom and coal-
cellar for Digory's cottage.

> 66 Gain all you can by using in your
> business all the understanding which God
> has given... 55 *John Wesley*

Opposite: (top)
John Wesley
preaches at
Gwennap Pit,
Cornwall;

(bottom)
modern open-
air witness at
Gwennap Pit.

Gwennap Pit,

near Redruth

This great hollow, created by the falling in of ancient mine workings, was used by Wesley as a preaching arena on eighteen occasions, the last when he was eighty-six years of age. He described it as 'a round green hollow, gently shelving down about fifty feet, two hundred feet across one way, three hundred feet across the other. I believe there were full 20,000 people, and the evening being calm, all could hear.'

Wesley recorded an even greater congregation in 1773: 'about two and thirty thousand people; the largest assembly I ever preached to. Yet I found all could hear, even to the skirts of the congregation. Perhaps the first time a man of seventy has been heard by thirty thousand persons at once.'

Today the amphitheatre is 116 feet in diameter, and twenty-six feet deep. It has thirteen tiers of turfed seats, eighteen inches high and three-and-a-half feet wide; two stumps of granite mark the spot where Wesley is believed to have stood to preach. Today regular services and other events are held here during the summer months.

A nearby chapel, built in 1836, now houses an exhibition of World Methodism, together with a snack bar and souvenir shop. Display boards tell the story of Wesley and Gwennap Pit.

This ash tree at Winchelsea replaced the original under which Wesley preached his last sermon.

John Wesley's last outdoor sermon, at Winchelsea, Sussex.

Opposite: The
Oak House,
West Bromwich,
visited by John
Wesley during
his travels.

The Midlands

Francis Asbury's House,

Newton Road, Great Barr
Francis Asbury, pioneer of American
Methodism, was born in Handsworth in 1745.
The house where he was brought up is now
preserved by the local authority. For more than
fifty years services were held in its front room.
It is now a memorial to the man who, more
than any other, created American Methodism.

A gentleman with bad eggs

"Between twelve and one, I preached at
Freshford... I had designed to preach there
again the next evening; but a gentleman in the
town desired me to preach at his door. The
beasts of the people were tolerably quiet till I
had nearly finished my sermon. They then
lifted up their voice, especially one, called a
gentleman, who had filled his pockets with rot-
ten eggs: but, a young man coming unawares,
clapped his hands on each side, and mashed
them all at once. In an instant he was perfume
all over; though it was not so sweet as balsam."

Wesley's Journal, 19 September 1769

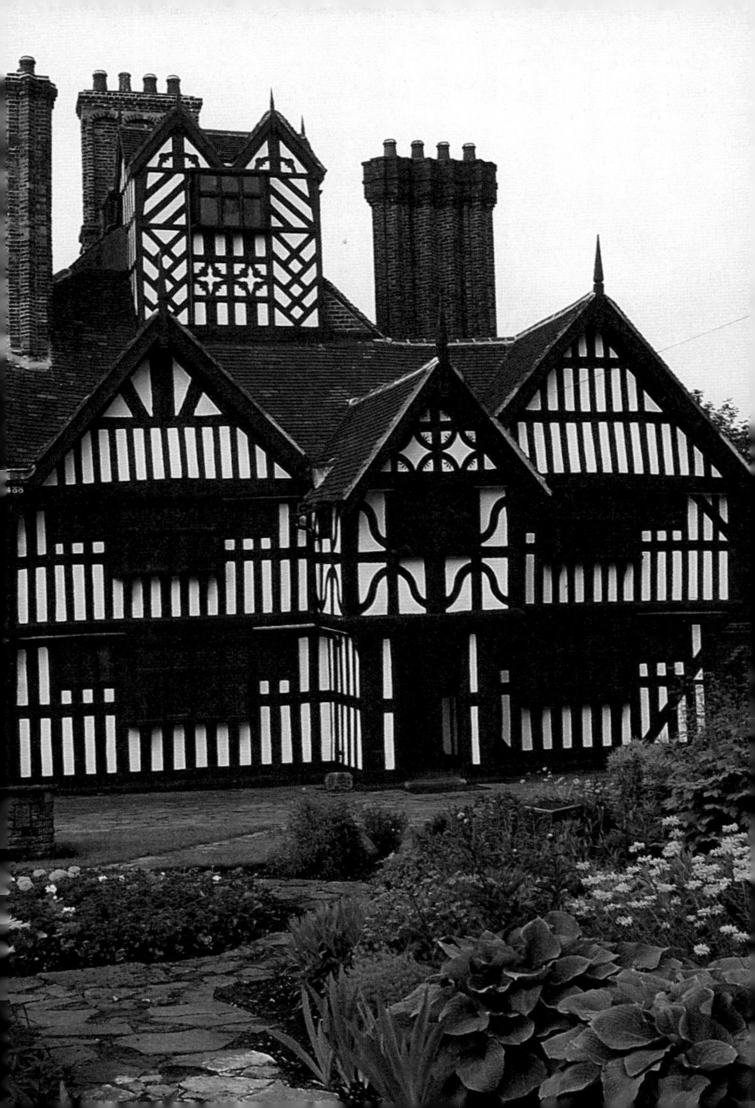

Jesus, lover of my soul

Jesus, lover of my soul,
let me to your presence fly,
while the gathering waters roll,
while the tempest still is high.
Hide me, O my Saviour, hide,
till the storm of life is past;
safe into the haven, guide
and receive my soul at last.

Other refuge have I none,
all my hope in you I see:
leave, O leave me, not alone;
still support and comfort me.
All my trust on you is stayed,
all my help from you I bring:
cover my defenceless head
with the shadow of your wing.

Plenteous grace with you is found,
grace to wash away my sin:
let the healing streams abound;
make and keep me clean within.
Living Fountain, now impart
all your life and purity;
spring for ever in my heart,
rise to all eternity!

Charles Wesley

Yorkshire

Wesley visited Yorkshire on many occasions, and Methodism has continued to thrive in this northern county.

The Preachers' House,

Heptonstall
Wesley visited Heptonstall regularly, and 4, Northgate, a double-fronted cottage still called 'The Preachers' Cottage', was where the local Methodist Society first met. It is marked today by a commemorative plaque.

The Heptonstall Chapel, sited in its own sloping, crowded graveyard, is a good example of early Methodist architecture. The roof was supplied from Rotherham, but the rest of the building was constructed by local craftsmen.

Osmotherley Chapel

Thirty miles north of York lies the moorland village of Osmotherley. The little stone meeting-house, hidden up a cobbled path, is one of the oldest Methodist chapels in the world.

The old chapel fell into disuse when a larger building was opened in 1864. However now the Victorian chapel has in its turn fallen into disuse, and the older chapel, more suited to the small congregations of the late twentieth century, has been restored as a memorial to Wesley.

The Society Book has also survived, by a

remarkable escape. It was once accidentally thrown onto a fire, but narrowly rescued from destruction. The book faithfully records the many times that John Wesley visited Osmotherley Chapel and preached to the villagers.

The Octagon Chapel,

Yarm

Yarm boasts the oldest Methodist octagon chapel in the world that is still in use by Methodists. It dates from 1763, and is also the second oldest chapel to be in continuous use for Methodist worship. It is situated in an alley at the side of the National Westminster Bank, in Yarm High Street.

'Love Divine All Loves Excelling' in Charles Wesley's own handwriting.

The original building of small red bricks has had its walls heightened and a gallery and

organ added, together with outer vestries and
rooms. The original pulpit has also been
replaced. A new entrance was added to the
chapel in 1963.

**❝ Once in seven years I burn all my
sermons; for it is a shame if I cannot write
better sermons now than I did seven
years ago. ❞**

John Wesley

Opposite:
Stained glass
depiction of
John Wesley
preaching, from
Wesley's
House.

County Durham

Newbiggin Chapel

At Newbiggin, in Teesdale, stands the oldest
existing Methodist chapel in continuous use
since Wesley's time. The chapel was first
erected in 1759/60, and enlarged in 1860. It
stands above the Alston road, which runs up
the dale, opposite the post office and on the
old road to the lead mines.

The chapel is a sturdy stone building, with a
stepped floor and a dozen varnished pews. A
long-funnelled coke stove dominates the interior. The present pulpit, pipe-organ and some
of the other furniture have been brought from
Bowlees Primitive Methodist chapel.

A pulpit used by John Wesley stands in one
corner; this was brought from Field Head, the
farm where Newbiggin Methodism began. Standing on the simple communion table are two
love-feast cups. Newbiggin Chapel originally
cost some sixty pounds to build, and had fifty-
seven founder members.

Wesley on democracy

❝The greater the share people have in
government, the less liberty, civil or religious,
does a nation enjoy.❞

John Wesley

And can it be that I should gain?

And can it be that I should gain
　　An interest in the Saviour's blood?
Died he for me, who caused his pain?
　　For me, who him to death pursued?
Amazing love! how can it be
That thou, my God, shouldst die for me!

'Tis mystery all! The Immortal dies:
　　Who can explore his strange design?
In vain the first-born seraph tries
　　To sound the depths of love divine.
'Tis mercy all! let earth adore,
Let angel minds inquire no more.

Long my imprisoned spirit lay
　　Fast bound in sin and nature's night;
Thine eye diffused a quickening ray –
　　I woke, the dungeon flamed with light;
My chains fell off, my heart was free,
I rose, went forth, and followed thee.

No condemnation now I dread;
　　Jesus, and all in him, is mine!
Alive in him, my living Head,
　　And clothed in righteousness divine,
Bold I approach the eternal throne,
And claim the crown, through Christ, my own.

Charles Wesley

Famous English Methodists

W.E.Sangster (1900-1960)
Sangster was a renowned evangelist and preacher, particularly during and immediately after World War II. He attracted great crowds during his sixteen years' ministry at Westminster Central Hall, London.

Jabez Bunting (1779-1858)
An early Methodist preacher and administrator, Jabez Bunting was secretary of the Methodist Conference, four times its president, and secretary of the missionary society. He more than any one else shaped Wesleyan Methodism.

T.B. Stephenson (1839-1912)
Stephenson, a Victorian Methodist minister in Lambeth, was appalled by the plight of homeless children, and started what has become the National Children's Home.

Hugh Price Hughes(1847-1902)
Founder of the *Methodist Times,* and of the inner-city missions and central halls.

George Thomas, Lord Tonypandy
Best-loved of recent Speakers of the House of Commons, lifelong Methodist and energetic lay-preacher. Lord Tonypandy has devoted his retirement to charitable works.

Lord Soper
continues
Wesley's
tradition of
open-air
preaching, at
Tower Hill,
London.

Lord Soper
Lord Soper, formerly minister of Kingsway Hall, has become world-famous for his open-air preaching on Tower Hill and at Speakers' Corner, Hyde Park. He is the first Methodist minister to sit in the House of Lords. As minister of Kingsway Hall, he followed such famous preachers as Hugh Price Hughes and J.Ernest Rattenbury.

Francis Asbury (1745-1816)

Francis Asbury was born into a Christian family in Birmingham, England, and experienced an evangelical conversion as a young teenager. He was poorly educated, and was apprenticed to a trade. Asbury joined the Methodists at an early age, and served as a travelling preacher 1766-71.

Asbury then responded to John Wesley's appeal for preachers to go to North America. He was an energetic itinerant preacher, the only one of Wesley's preachers to stay in the colonies during the Revolutionary War. In 1784 Francis Asbury and Thomas Coke were named as joint superintendents of the Methodist Societies in the United States.

Against Wesley's wishes, Asbury took the title of bishop. Since Thomas Coke was frequently away, it was Asbury who was largely responsible for shaping American Methodism. He was often sick, but nevertheless covered almost 300,000 miles on horseback during his ministry, much of it on the barren frontiers of the United States.

Wesley on slavery

❝...Go on, in the name of God and in the power of his might, till even American slavery, the vilest that ever saw the sun, shall vanish before it... **❞**

From his last letter, to William Wilberforce, in 1791

Some Wesley Facts and Figures

John Wesley preached more than 40,000 sermons.
John Wesley was only five feet three inches tall and weighed only 128 pounds.
Charles Wesley wrote more than 6,500 hymns.
John Wesley was one of eighteen children.
John Wesley published about 500 books, sermons, tracts and pamphlets.
During his ministry John Wesley covered more than 250,000 miles on horseback .
At his death, Wesley's followers numbered 79,000 in England and 40,000 in North America.

John Wesley in old age.

John Wesley's Spiritual Journey

Wednesday, May 24, 1738

What occurred on Wednesday May 24, 1738,
I think best to relate at large, after premising what
may make it the better understood. Let him that
cannot receive it, ask of the Father of lights, that
he would give more light to him and me.

1. I believe, till I was about ten years old, I had not
sinned away that *Washing of the Holy Ghost* which
was given me in baptism, having been strictly
educated and carefully taught, that I could only be
saved *by universal obedience, by keeping all the
commandments of God;* in the meaning of which
I was diligently instructed. And those instructions,
so far as they respected outward duties and sins,
I gladly received, and often thought of. But all that
was said to me of inward obedience, or holiness,
I neither understood nor remembered. So that
I was indeed as ignorant of the true meaning of the
law as I was of the Gospel of Christ.

2. The next six or seven years were spent at
school; where outward restraints being removed,
I was much more negligent than before even of
outward duties, and almost continually guilty of
outward sins, which I knew to be such, though
they were not scandalous in the eye of the world.
However I still read the Scriptures, and said my
prayers morning and evening. And what I now
hoped to be saved by was, 1. *Not being so bad as
other people.* 2. *Having still a kindness for*

religion. And 3. *Reading the Bible, going to church, and saying my prayers.*

3. Being removed to the university, for five years, I still said my prayers both in public and private, and read with my Scriptures several other books of religion, especially comments on the New Testament. Yet I had not all this while so much as a notion of inward holiness; nay, went on habitually, and, for the most part, very contentedly, in some or other known sin: Indeed with some intermissions and short struggles, especially before and after the Holy Communion, which I was obliged to receive thrice a year. I cannot well tell what I hoped to be saved by now, when I was continually sinning against that little light I had; unless by those transient fits of what many divines taught me to call *Repentance.*

4. When I was about twenty-two, my father pressed me to enter into Holy Orders. At the same time the Providence of God directing me to *Kempis's Christian Pattern,* I began to see that true Religion was seated in the heart, and that God's law extended to all our thoughts as well as words and actions. I was however very angry at Kempis for being *too strict,* though I read him only in Dean Stanhope's translation. Yet I had frequently much sensible comfort in reading him, such as I was an utter stranger to before. And meeting likewise with a religious friend, which I never had until now, I began to alter the whole form of my conversation, and to set in earnest upon a *New Life.* I set apart an hour or two a day for religious retirement. I communicated every week. I watched against all sin, whether in word or deed. I began to aim at and pray for inward holiness. So that now, *doing so much, and living so good a life,* I doubted not but I was a good Christian.

5. Removing soon to another College, I executed a resolution, which I was before convinced was of the utmost importance, shaking off at once all my trifling acquaintance. I began to see more and more the value of time. I applied myself closer to study. I watched more carefully against actual sins: I advised others to be religious, according to the scheme of religion by which I modeled my own life. But meeting now with with Mr. Law's *Christian Perfection and Serious Call* (although I was much offended at many parts of both, yet) they convinced me more than ever of the exceeding height, and breadth, and depth of the law of God. The light flowed in so mightily upon my soul that everything appeared in a new view. I cried to God for help, and resolved not to prolong the time of obeying him as I had never done before. And by my continued *endeavour to keep his whole law,* inward and outward, *to the utmost of my power,* I was persuaded that I should be accepted of him, and that I was even then in a state of salvation.

6. In 1730, I began visiting the prisons, assisting the poor and sick in town, and doing what other good I could by my presence, or my little fortune, to the bodies and souls of all men. To this end I abridged myself of all superfluities, and many that are called necessities of life. I soon became *a by-word* for so doing, and I rejoiced that *my name was cast out as evil.* The next Spring I began observing the Wednesday and Friday Fasts, commonly observed in the ancient church; tasting no food until three in the afternoon. And now

I knew not how to go any further. I diligently strove against all sin. I omitted no sort of self-denial which I thought lawful; I carefully used, both in public and in private, all the means of grace at all opportunities. I omitted no occasion of doing good. I for that reason suffered evil. And all this I knew to be nothing, unless it was directed toward inward holiness. Accordingly this (the image of God) was what I aimed at in all, by doing his will, not my own. Yet when after continuing some years in this course, I apprehended myself to be near death, I could not find that all this gave me any comfort, or any assurance of acceptance with God. At this I was not then a little surprised; not imagining I had been all this time building on the sand, (not so; I was right as far as I went) not considering that *other foundation can no man lay than that which is laid by God, even* Christ Jesus.

7. Soon after a contemplative man convinced me still more than I was convinced before, that outward works are nothing, being alone: and in several conversations instructed me how to pursue inward holiness, or a union of the soul with God. But even of his instructions, though I then received them as the words of God, I cannot but now observe. 1. That he spoke so incautiously against *trusting* in *outward works,* that he discouraged me from *doing* them at all. 2. That he recommended, as it were to supply what was wanting in them, *mental prayer,* and the like exercises, as the most effectual means of purifying the soul, and uniting it with God. Now these were in truth, as much *my own works* as visiting the sick or clothing the naked, and the *union with* God thus pursued, was as really *my own unrighteousness,* as any I had before pursued, under another name.

8. In this *refined* way of trusting to my own works and my own righteousness, so zealously inculcated by the *Mystic* writers, I dragged on heavily, finding no comfort or help therein, till the time of my leaving England. On shipboard, however, I was again active in outward works: where it pleased God, of his free mercy, to give me twenty-six of the Moravian brethren for companions, who endeavoured to shew me a more excellent way. But I understood it not at first. I was too learned and too wise; so that it seemed foolishness unto me. And I continued... trusting in that righteousness whereby no flesh can be justified.

9. All the time I was at Savannah I was thus *beating the air.* Being ignorant of the righteousness of Christ, which, by a living faith in him bringeth salvation *to every one that believeth,* I sought to establish my own righteousness, and so laboured in the fire all my days. I was now, properly *under the Law;* I knew that "the Law of God was spiritual;" "I consented to it that it was good. Yea, I delighted in it, after the inner man." Yet I was "carnal, sold under sin." Every day I was constrained to cry out, "What I do, I allow not; for what I would I do not, but what I hate, that I do. To will is indeed present with me; but how to perform that which is good, I find not. For the good which I would, I do not; but the evil which I would not, that I do. I find a law, that when I would do good, evil is present with me: Even the law in my members warring against the law of my mind, and still bringing me into captivity to the law of sin."

10. In this state, I was indeed fighting continually, but not conquering. Before, I had willingly served sin; now it was unwillingly, but still I served it. I fell and rose, and fell again. Sometimes I was overcome, and in heaviness: Sometimes I overcome, and was in joy. For, as in the former state, I had some foretastes of the terrors of the Law, so had I in this, of the comforts of the Gospel. During this whole struggle between nature and grace, which had now continued above ten years, I had many remarkable returns to prayer, especially when I was in trouble: I had many sensible comforts, which are indeed no other than short anticipations of the life of faith. But I was still *under the Law,* not *under Grace,* the state most who are called Christians are content to live and die in. For I was only *striving with,* not *freed from* sin: Neither had I *the witness of the Spirit with my spirit.* And indeed could not: for "I sought it not by faith, but, as it were, by the works of the Law."

11. In my return to England, January 1738, being in imminent danger of death, and very uneasy on that account, I was strongly convinced that the cause of that uneasiness was unbelief, and that the gaining a true, living faith was the *one thing needful for me.* But still I fixt not this faith on its right object: I meant only faith in God, not faith in or through Christ. Again, I know not that I was *wholly void of this faith;* but only thought, *I had not enough of it.* So that when Peter Boehler, whom God prepared for me as soon as I came to London, affirmed of true faith in Christ, which is but one, that it had those two fruits inseparably attending it, "Dominion over sin, and constant peace from a sense of forgiveness," I was quite

amazed, and looked upon it as a new Gospel.
If this were so, it was clear I had not faith...

12. ...they added with one mouth, that this faith
was the gift, the free gift of God, and that he would
surely bestow it upon every soul, who earnestly
and perseveringly sought it. I was not thoroughly
convinced; and, by the grace of God, I resolved to
seek it unto the end. 1. By absolutely renouncing
all dependence, in whole or in part, upon *my own*
works or righteousness, on which I had really
grounded my hope of salvation, though I knew it
not, from my youth up. 2. By adding to *the
constant use of all the* other *means of grace,*
continual prayer for this very thing, justifying,
saving faith, a full reliance on the blood of Christ,
shed for *me;* a trust in him, *as my* Christ, as *my*
sole justification, sanctification and redemption...

13. In the evening, I went very unwillingly to a
Society in Aldersgate-Street, where one was
reading Luther's preface to the Epistle to the
Romans. About a quarter before nine, while he
was describing the change which God works in the
heart through faith in Christ, I felt my heart
strangely warmed. I felt I did trust in Christ; Christ
alone, for salvation; and an assurance was given
me, that he had taken away *my* sins, even *mine,*
and saved *me* from the law of sin and death.

14. I began to pray with all my might for those who
had in a more especial manner despitefully used
me and persecuted me. I then testified openly to
all there, what I now first felt in my heart. But it was
not long before the enemy suggested, ''This
cannot be Faith; for where is thy joy?'' Then was I
taught, that ''Peace and victory over sin, are

This grateful Record
of the place made sacred by the
Mortal Remains
of the Venerable and Apostolic
WESLEY
was first erected A·D·MDCCXCI

IN THIS VAULT WITH THE REMAINS OF
THE REVᴰ Mʳ WESLEY
ARE DEPOSITED THOSE OF THE FOLLOWING MINISTERS
Mʳ DUNCAN WRIGHT DIED MAY 15ᵀᴴ 1791 AGED 55 YEARS
Revᴰ JOHN RICHARDSON DIED FEB 8ᵀᴴ 1792 AGED 61 YEARS
Mʳ JOHN MURLIN DIED JULY 7ᵀᴴ 1799 AGED 77 YEARS
Revᴰ WALTER GRIFFITH { DIED JANᵞ 30ᵀᴴ 1826 AGED 63 YEARS
PRESIDENT OF THE
CONFERENCE 1815
ALSO Rᴇᴠ. THOMAS OLIVERS, BORN 1726. DIED MARCH 1799.
CORRECTOR OF THE PRESS OF Mʳ WESLEY.
AUTHOR OF THE HYMN "THE GOD OF ABRAHAM PRAISE"
AND THE TUNE CALLED HELMSLEY.

ESLEY
1791

essential to Faith in the Captain of our salvation: But, that as to the transports of joy that usually attend the beginning of it, especially in those who had mourned deeply, God sometimes giveth, sometimes with-holdeth them, according to the counsels of his own will.''

15. After my return home, I was much buffeted with temptations: But cried out, and they fled away. They returned again and again. I as often lifted up my eyes, and he ''sent me help from his holy place.'' And herein I found the difference between this and my former state chiefly consisted. I was striving, yea, fighting with all my might under the law, as well as under grace. But then I was sometimes, if not often, conquered; now, I was always conqueror.

John Wesley's Journal

Further reading

Cyril Davey: *John Wesley and the Methodists*

Frederick C. Gill: *Charles Wesley, the First Methodist*

William Leary and John Vickers: *A Methodist Guide to Lincolnshire and East Anglia*

John Vickers and Betty Young: *A Methodist Guide to London and the South-East*

John Wesley's *Forty-four Sermons*

John Wesley's *Journal*

Photograph acknowledgments

T. E. Dowley: 19, 23, 24, 27, 80, 82, 85, 87, 88, 90
Mary Evans Picture Library: 39, 98 (top)
National Portrait Gallery: 9
John Rylands University Library of Manchester and the Methodist Church Archives and History Committee: 59, 106
Clifford Shirley: 95
Thomas Photos, Oxford: 33
Morris Walker: 13, 18, 25, 26, 31 (both), 56, 83, 94, 98 (bottom), 100 (both), 103, 115
Peter Wyart: 7, 29, 35, 40, 43, 44, 45, 46, 47, 50, 52, 53, 54, 55, 56, 60, 61, 62, 65, 66, 69, 70, 73, 74, 76, 78, 79, 84, 97, 107, 108, 110, 12 3

Maps
James Macdonald: Plan of Lincoln College; maps of Oxford and London

Richard Scott: Map of Great Britain

We are grateful to the Trustees of Wesley's Chapel, London, to John Wesley's Chapel, Broadmead, Bristol, and to the Methodist Church Overseas Division for permission to reproduce photographs of paintings in their possession.

Names and addresses of tour companions